iOS 18.4 Mastery

Everything You Need to Know About Apple's Latest Features and Enhancements

SOPHIA O. RAVENN

TABLE OF CONTENTS

INTRODUCTION

Apple's iOS 18.4 isn't just another routine update—it's a game-changer. With every new iteration, Apple pushes the boundaries of innovation, refining the iPhone experience to make it smarter, faster, and more intuitive. But iOS 18.4 goes beyond mere refinements; it introduces powerful enhancements that reshape how users interact with their devices. Whether you're a casual iPhone user, a tech enthusiast, or someone who wants to unlock every hidden feature, this update is designed to elevate your experience in ways you never imagined.

What makes iOS 18.4 stand out? It's not just about bug fixes or minor performance tweaks—this update brings meaningful changes that redefine customization, security, and functionality. Apple has introduced enhancements that give users greater control over their devices, from privacy-focused updates to seamless multitasking improvements. The user interface feels more refined, apps respond with unprecedented efficiency, and new features integrate so naturally into your daily routine that they feel like they've always been there.

This guide is your roadmap to mastering iOS 18.4, ensuring that you don't just scratch the surface but dive deep into everything this update has to offer. Whether you want to maximize productivity, enhance privacy, or simply make your iPhone more efficient, this book will walk you through every change, feature, and hidden trick. It's designed for both beginners who need step-by-step guidance and advanced users eager to discover the lesser-known aspects of iOS 18.4.

By the time you turn the last page, you won't just be using iOS 18.4—you'll be mastering it. So, get ready to unlock the full potential of your iPhone and transform the way you interact with your device. The journey starts now.

Chapter 1

Getting Started with iOS 18.4

With every iOS update, Apple refines its ecosystem to enhance performance, security, and user experience. iOS 18.4 is no exception. Whether you're upgrading from an older iOS version or setting up a new device, understanding the process is crucial to ensure a smooth transition. From checking compatibility to preparing your iPhone for the update, this chapter will guide you through every step to ensure that you get the best experience with iOS 18.4.

Devices Compatible with iOS 18.4

Before diving into the update process, the first step is to confirm whether your device supports iOS 18.4. Apple typically extends software support to a wide range of iPhone models, ensuring that even older devices benefit from security patches and performance improvements. However, as iOS evolves, some older models may lose compatibility due to hardware limitations.

If you're using an iPhone released within the last five to six years, chances are your device is eligible for iOS 18.4. To verify compatibility, navigate to **Settings > General > About** and check your iPhone model. Additionally, Apple's official website lists all supported devices for each iOS release.

Here's a list of devices expected to support iOS 18.4:

- **iPhone 16 Pro Max, iPhone 16 Pro, iPhone 16, iPhone 16 Plus**
- **iPhone 15 Pro Max, iPhone 15 Pro, iPhone 15, iPhone 15 Plus**
- **iPhone 14 Pro Max, iPhone 14 Pro, iPhone 14, iPhone 14 Plus**
- **iPhone 13 Pro Max, iPhone 13 Pro, iPhone 13, iPhone 13 Mini**
- **iPhone 12 Pro Max, iPhone 12 Pro, iPhone 12, iPhone 12 Mini**
- **iPhone 11 Pro Max, iPhone 11 Pro, iPhone 11**
- **iPhone SE (2nd generation and later)**

If your device is listed above, you're eligible for the iOS 18.4 update. If not, it may be time to consider upgrading to a newer model to continue enjoying Apple's latest features and security updates.

How to Update to iOS 18.4

Updating to iOS 18.4 is a straightforward process, and Apple provides two primary methods to install the latest software: **Over-the-Air (OTA) Update** and **Manual Update via iTunes or Finder**.

Method 1: Over-the-Air (OTA) Update

This is the simplest way to update your iPhone, directly from the device itself.

1. **Connect to Wi-Fi** – Ensure your iPhone is connected to a stable Wi-Fi network to avoid data interruptions.

2. **Check Battery Level** – Your device should have at least **50% battery** or be plugged into a power source.

3. **Go to Settings** – Open **Settings > General > Software Update**.

4. **Download and Install** – If iOS 18.4 is available, tap **Download and Install**. Follow the on-screen instructions.

5. **Restart Your iPhone** – Once the installation is complete, your iPhone will restart to apply the update.

Method 2: Manual Update via iTunes or Finder

If you experience issues with the OTA method or prefer a clean install, updating through a computer is an alternative.

1. **Connect Your iPhone** – Use a USB cable to connect your iPhone to a Mac or Windows PC.
2. **Open Finder (Mac) or iTunes (Windows)** – If using a Mac with macOS Catalina or later, open **Finder**. If using an older Mac or Windows PC, open **iTunes**.
3. **Select Your Device** – Click on your iPhone in the sidebar.
4. **Check for Updates** – Click **Check for Update** and if iOS 18.4 is

available, select **Download and Install**.

5. **Follow On-Screen Instructions –** The process may take a few minutes. Once completed, your iPhone will restart.

Essential Steps Before Updating

Before jumping into the installation, certain preparatory steps are essential to avoid any issues and ensure that your data remains safe.

1. Backup Your iPhone

Backing up your data is crucial to prevent data loss in case of an update failure. There are two primary ways to back up your device:

- **iCloud Backup:**

    1. Go to **Settings > [Your Name] > iCloud > iCloud Backup**.
    2. Tap **Back Up Now** and wait for the process to complete.
    3. Ensure you have enough iCloud storage before proceeding.

- **Mac or PC Backup:**

    1. Connect your iPhone to a Mac or Windows PC.
    2. Open **Finder (Mac) or iTunes (Windows)**.
    3. Click on your device and select **Back Up Now**.
    4. Wait for the backup to finish before updating.

2. Check Available Storage

iOS updates require a certain amount of free space for installation. To check your storage:

1. Go to **Settings > General > iPhone Storage**.
2. Review the space available and delete unnecessary apps or media if needed.
3. Aim for at least **5GB of free storage** for a smooth update process.

3. Ensure Your Apple ID and Password Are Ready

After updating, your iPhone may ask for your Apple ID credentials to complete the setup. If

you don't remember your password, reset it
before updating.

4. Update Apps

Some apps may require updates to function
properly on iOS 18.4. To update them:

1. Open the **App Store**.
2. Tap on your profile picture.
3. Select **Update All** to ensure all your
   apps are optimized for iOS 18.4.

Understanding the Installation Process

Once the update is downloaded, your iPhone
will automatically begin the installation.
Here's what to expect:

Step 1: Preparing for Installation

- The update will verify the file integrity before installation begins.
- Your device may require a restart to proceed.

Step 2: Installation Process

- The iPhone screen will turn black with the Apple logo and a progress bar.
- Installation time varies depending on your device and internet speed.

Step 3: Post-Installation Setup

Once the installation is complete, your iPhone will restart, and you'll see the **Hello** screen. Follow these steps:

1. **Enter Your Passcode** – If you use Face ID or Touch ID, re-enter your passcode.
2. **Sign In to Your Apple ID** – You may be required to log in with your Apple ID.
3. **Check App Compatibility** – Open essential apps to ensure they work smoothly with iOS 18.4.
4. **Review New Features** – Visit **Settings > General > About** to see the new version and explore the latest changes.

Updating to iOS 18.4 is a straightforward process, but preparation is key to ensuring a hassle-free experience. By backing up your device, checking compatibility, and following the right installation method, you can enjoy all the latest enhancements without any issues. With the update complete, it's time to explore the exciting features that iOS 18.4 has to offer.

Chapter 2

Exploring the New Features

Apple continues to push the boundaries of innovation with each iOS update, and iOS 18.4 is no exception. This latest version introduces a range of exciting features, refined user interface tweaks, and system-wide improvements that enhance both functionality and aesthetics. From everyday usability enhancements to performance optimizations, iOS 18.4 builds upon its predecessors to deliver a smoother, faster, and more intuitive experience.

For users upgrading from an earlier version, the transition will feel seamless, yet they'll notice meaningful upgrades that impact how they interact with their devices. Whether it's the refined visuals, upgraded system apps, or improvements in speed and stability, iOS 18.4 is designed to optimize the iPhone experience.

Major Improvements and Enhancements

One of the standout changes in iOS 18.4 is the improved **AI-powered functionalities** integrated across various aspects of the operating system. Apple has significantly enhanced **Siri's intelligence**, allowing it to process more complex requests, maintain conversation continuity, and perform advanced in-app functions. Siri now better understands user intent, making interactions more natural and efficient.

Another key enhancement is **real-time translation and dictation improvements**. The on-device AI has been upgraded to support more languages with improved accuracy, making translations smoother and faster. Users who rely on voice typing will experience fewer errors and better autocorrection, further streamlining text input across all applications.

Additionally, **Live Captions** have been enhanced, providing **real-time subtitles** for media playback, FaceTime calls, and even in-person conversations. This feature makes accessibility even more inclusive, allowing those with hearing impairments to follow along effortlessly.

Apple has also introduced **adaptive display adjustments** that dynamically adjust color balance, contrast, and brightness based on the surrounding environment. This enhancement ensures that content remains easily visible regardless of lighting conditions, reducing eye strain and improving usability in different settings.

Design Tweaks and UI Refinements

Apple has always been known for its clean, user-friendly design, and iOS 18.4 introduces several UI refinements that enhance visual appeal and ease of navigation. One of the most noticeable changes is the **lock screen**

customization enhancements, allowing users to apply more advanced widgets, interactive wallpapers, and real-time notifications without unlocking their devices.

Control Center customization has also been expanded, enabling users to rearrange and resize toggles for a more personalized experience. The ability to **group settings** into folders within the Control Center provides quick access to commonly used functions without cluttering the interface.

Apple has also redesigned **notification grouping**, making it easier to manage multiple alerts by intelligently categorizing them based on priority. Users can now set **custom notification sounds and vibrations** for different apps, ensuring that they can differentiate between important alerts and routine messages with ease.

The **app switcher interface** has been fine-tuned for better multitasking, allowing users to **preview running apps in larger windows** before selecting them. This improvement makes it easier to navigate between tasks while maintaining a smooth transition from one app to another.

For users who prefer dark mode, iOS 18.4 has introduced **adaptive dark mode**, which automatically adjusts **contrast levels based on screen brightness**. This makes reading in low-light conditions more comfortable without sacrificing visibility in well-lit environments.

Upgrades in System Apps and Usability

Many of Apple's built-in apps have received significant updates, improving both functionality and ease of use.

- **Messages**: The **Messages app** now supports **message scheduling**, allowing users to send texts at a later time. Additionally, Apple has enhanced **Tapback reactions**, adding more emoji responses and allowing users to create custom reactions. Group chat features have also been expanded, making it easier to manage conversations with multiple participants.

- **Safari**: The **Safari browser** has been optimized for **faster page loading**, improved tab management, and **better privacy controls**. Apple has introduced **AI-powered content summarization**, which automatically highlights key points from articles, saving users time while browsing.

- **Mail**: The Mail app has received new features, including **smart filtering**, which automatically categorizes emails based on priority. Users can also take advantage of **AI-powered auto-replies**, which suggest responses based on context.

- **Notes & Reminders**: Notes now supports **handwriting recognition with Apple Pencil**, allowing users to convert handwritten notes into text. Additionally, **voice recordings can be transcribed in real-time**, making it easier to capture thoughts on the go. Reminders have been enhanced with **location-based triggers**, sending alerts when users arrive at specific locations.

- **Camera & Photos**: The **Camera app** has been upgraded with **improved night mode**, better AI-driven scene detection, and a **pro-level manual mode** for advanced users. The Photos app now uses **AI-based sorting**, automatically categorizing images into collections for easier navigation. Users can also take advantage of **video background removal**, allowing them to edit videos with greater precision.

- **Apple Maps**: **Apple Maps** now includes **augmented reality navigation**, providing real-world overlays that help users navigate more intuitively. Live traffic updates have been improved, and users can **download offline maps** for navigation without an internet connection.

- **Health & Fitness**: The **Health app** now features **customized workout**

suggestions, more accurate sleep tracking, and **medication reminders** with integration into Apple Watch. The Fitness app offers **AI-driven coaching**, recommending personalized fitness plans based on user activity history.

Performance Improvements and System Stability

iOS 18.4 isn't just about visual and functional upgrades; it also focuses heavily on **performance optimizations** that enhance overall stability and responsiveness.

Speed Enhancements: Apple has optimized the system kernel to **reduce app**

launch times, making everyday tasks feel noticeably faster. Users will experience smoother animations and **quicker app switching**, even on older devices.

Battery Efficiency: Battery life remains a priority, and iOS 18.4 includes **adaptive power management** that intelligently adjusts background processes based on usage patterns. This helps extend battery life, especially for users who rely on their devices throughout the day.

System Stability: Apple has addressed multiple background processes to **reduce system crashes and app freezes**. Memory management improvements ensure that even **resource-intensive applications run more smoothly** without excessive battery drain.

Connectivity Improvements: iOS 18.4 features **enhanced Wi-Fi stability** and **faster 5G performance**, ensuring that users experience **fewer dropped connections and improved data speeds**. Bluetooth connectivity has also been refined for **more stable connections with accessories**, including AirPods and third-party devices.

Apple has also integrated **AI-powered app optimization**, allowing iOS to intelligently allocate resources to the apps that need them most. This ensures that even high-performance applications like **video editing software or advanced gaming apps** run efficiently without compromising speed.

The improvements introduced in iOS 18.4 highlight Apple's commitment to refining user experience, making devices faster, more efficient, and packed with innovative features. The UI refinements ensure better usability, while system app enhancements bring powerful new tools to everyday users. Performance and stability improvements make sure that every interaction feels smooth, regardless of the device being used.

For those who rely on their iPhones for productivity, communication, and entertainment, iOS 18.4 provides a well-rounded update that enhances every aspect of the device. Whether it's the expanded Siri functionality, better multitasking features, or system-wide performance boosts, this update is designed to make your iPhone

smarter and more responsive than ever
before.

Chapter 3

Hidden Features & Customization

Apple consistently introduces new features with every iOS update, but not all of them receive the spotlight they deserve. While the major improvements in iOS 18.4 are widely discussed, there are numerous hidden gems that enhance usability, convenience, and personalization. These lesser-known features allow users to tailor their iPhones to suit their preferences, optimize functionality, and unlock a more efficient experience. This chapter uncovers these hidden features and provides guidance on how to customize the home screen, Control Center, widgets, and other personalization settings.

Lesser-Known Features and How to Unlock Them

Beyond the widely advertised upgrades, iOS 18.4 is packed with subtle yet powerful enhancements that can significantly impact how users interact with their devices. Here are some of the most noteworthy hidden features and how to activate them:

1. Back Tap Shortcuts – Now More Powerful

Apple's **Back Tap** feature, which allows users to trigger actions by tapping the back of their iPhone, has been upgraded with additional customization options. Users can now assign **triple-tap gestures** to perform advanced shortcuts, such as launching specific apps, taking screenshots, toggling low power mode, or even executing Siri Shortcuts.

- **How to enable:**
    1. Go to **Settings** > **Accessibility** > **Touch**.
    2. Scroll down to **Back Tap** and choose **Double Tap** or **Triple Tap**.
    3. Select an action or shortcut to assign to each gesture.

2. Secret Safari Gesture for Quick Navigation

For those who frequently browse the web, Safari now supports a **hidden swipe gesture** to instantly switch between open tabs. By swiping **horizontally across the bottom of the screen**, users can move seamlessly from one tab to another, making multitasking more fluid.

- **How to enable:** This feature is enabled by default; simply use **a left or right swipe at the bottom of Safari** to navigate between tabs.

3. Custom App Icons Without Shortcuts Delay

Previously, using custom app icons required routing through the Shortcuts app, causing a brief delay when launching apps. iOS 18.4 removes this limitation, allowing **direct custom app icons** without interruptions. Users can now fully personalize their home screen aesthetic without the inconvenience of unnecessary loading screens.

- **How to enable:**
  1. Press and hold an app icon on the home screen.
  2. Select **Edit Home Screen**, then tap the app.
  3. Choose **Change Icon** and select from a preset gallery or upload your own image.

4.   Interactive   Dynamic   Island Enhancements

Apple has expanded **Dynamic Island** functionality, allowing for **live tracking widgets** that integrate seamlessly with real-time activities. This means that sports scores, Uber rides, music playback, and even smart home controls can now be accessed directly from the Dynamic Island without opening apps.

- **How to enable:** Certain apps will automatically support this feature, but users can check app settings to configure live updates in **Settings** > **Dynamic Island Preferences**.

5. AI-Powered Auto-Categorization in Photos

The Photos app now leverages **on-device AI to automatically categorize images**

into smart albums, organizing them based on themes such as "Family Moments," "Landscapes," or "Screenshots." This makes searching for specific photos far more efficient.

- **How to enable:** This feature is enabled by default, but users can manually adjust sorting preferences in **Settings** > **Photos**.

Customizing Home Screen, Control Center, and Widgets

One of the most exciting aspects of iOS 18.4 is the expanded **home screen customization options**, which allow users to create a more personalized and efficient interface.

1. Home Screen Customization

- **Advanced Widget Stacking:** Users can now create **intelligent widget stacks** that automatically rotate based on usage patterns.
- **Transparent App Icons:** A new setting allows users to make app icons partially transparent, blending them seamlessly into the wallpaper.
- **Themed Icon Packs:** Apple now offers built-in themed icon packs that match the system-wide color palette.

2. Control Center Personalization

The **Control Center** has been redesigned for greater customization, offering:

- **Resizable toggles:** Users can now adjust the size of shortcuts like brightness, volume, and connectivity controls.

- **Grouped settings:** Users can create **folders for Control Center toggles**, such as grouping Wi-Fi, Bluetooth, and Airplane Mode under a single swipe-down menu.

- **Live widgets:** Apps like Music and Smart Home now have **live updating widgets** in the Control Center, allowing for one-touch control without opening the full app.

- **How to customize:**

  1. Go to **Settings** > **Control Center**.

2. Tap **Customize Controls** to add, remove, or rearrange shortcuts.

3. Drag widgets to reorder or group them into categories.

3. Widget Customization

Widgets are now more interactive than ever, allowing for greater control and real-time information display.

- **Expanded Sizes:** Users can now place **larger, high-detail widgets** on the home screen.

- **Interactive Functionality:** Certain widgets now allow users to interact directly, such as checking off tasks from a **Reminders widget** or playing music without opening the app.

- **Dynamic Transparency:** Widgets can be set to dynamically adjust their transparency based on the background, creating a cleaner aesthetic.

- **How to customize widgets:**

  1. Press and hold an empty space on the home screen until the icons start to jiggle.
  2. Tap the + in the top left corner.
  3. Browse available widgets and select a size and type.
  4. Drag and place the widget in a preferred location.

Personalization Settings for Accessibility and User Experience

Apple remains committed to making iPhones as accessible as possible, and iOS 18.4 introduces several new **accessibility and user experience enhancements** that benefit all users, especially those with special needs.

1. Adaptive Touch Controls

For users who have difficulty with precise gestures, **Adaptive Touch Controls** allow for:

- Adjustable **touch sensitivity** for different screen areas.

- Customizable **gesture shortcuts** to trigger specific actions without requiring complex swipes.

- **How to enable:**

    1. Navigate to **Settings > Accessibility > Touch Accommodations**.
    2. Adjust the **hold duration, swipe sensitivity, and tap assistance** as needed.

2. Personalized Sound Enhancements

The **Live Listen feature** now provides **real-time sound adjustments** based on user hearing profiles, enhancing clarity for conversations and media playback.

- **How to enable:**
    1. Go to **Settings** > **Accessibility** > **Hearing** > **Live Listen**.
    2. Pair with AirPods or compatible Bluetooth devices for enhanced sound clarity.

3. Smart Automation Shortcuts

The Shortcuts app now allows for **AI-powered automation suggestions**, helping users streamline daily tasks by setting up **location-based or time-based actions**.

- **Example automations:**

    1. **Auto-silence notifications** when arriving at work.

2. **Enable Do Not Disturb** when starting a workout.
3. **Turn on Low Power Mode** when battery drops below 20%.

- **How to set up:**

1. Open **Shortcuts** app.
2. Tap **Automation > Create Personal Automation**.
3. Select a trigger (time, location, app usage).
4. Choose an action and customize settings.

iOS 18.4 goes beyond surface-level updates to provide users with a vast array of **hidden features and customization tools** that empower them to tailor their devices to their unique preferences. From advanced **gesture controls** and **home screen personalization** to **accessibility improvements** and **interactive widgets**, this update makes iPhones more adaptable than ever before.

Chapter 4

Security & Privacy Upgrades

With each iOS update, Apple reinforces its commitment to **privacy and security**, ensuring that users have greater control over their data and a more secure experience. iOS 18.4 introduces several **enhanced security measures, authentication upgrades, and privacy settings** that protect personal information while maintaining ease of access. As cyber threats evolve, Apple continues to implement **cutting-edge encryption, advanced authentication, and smarter app permissions** to keep user data safe. This chapter explores the latest security enhancements, including updates to **Face ID, passcodes, app tracking, and overall data protection**.

New Privacy Settings and Enhanced Security Measures

Privacy remains one of Apple's core values, and iOS 18.4 expands its suite of **privacy-focused tools** that give users more **transparency and control over their data**. These new features ensure that users know how their information is used and provide **greater safeguards against unauthorized access**.

1. Advanced Lockdown Mode for High-Risk Users

Apple introduced **Lockdown Mode** in previous versions of iOS for users at higher risk of cyberattacks, such as journalists, activists, and government officials. In iOS 18.4, this feature has been **enhanced with broader protection mechanisms**, including:

- **Stricter network security**, blocking unknown internet connections that may attempt to exploit vulnerabilities.

- **Tighter restrictions on unknown messages and links**, preventing malicious attempts via iMessage and email.

- **App execution control**, which limits apps from running unnecessary background processes.

- **How to enable:**

  1. Go to **Settings** > **Privacy & Security** > **Lockdown Mode**.
  2. Tap **Turn On Lockdown Mode**, review the warning, and confirm.

2. On-Device AI for Data Privacy

iOS 18.4 introduces **on-device AI processing**, ensuring that **sensitive data is analyzed locally rather than being sent to Apple's servers**. This applies to:

- **Siri requests**, keeping conversations private.
- **Photo analysis**, ensuring facial recognition and categorization happen on the device.
- **Keyboard and predictive text processing**, preventing typing patterns from being shared externally.

3. Enhanced Private Relay for Anonymous Browsing

Apple's **iCloud Private Relay** has been upgraded with **stronger encryption protocols**, preventing websites from tracking user activity while browsing Safari. This feature ensures that even **internet service providers and Apple cannot see what websites users visit**.

- **How to enable:**
    1. Open **Settings** > **iCloud** > **Private Relay**.
    2. Toggle **On** for a more private browsing experience.

Updates to Face ID, Passcodes, and Authentication Methods

Authentication plays a crucial role in securing an iPhone, and iOS 18.4 introduces **faster, more secure authentication methods** while making logins more convenient.

1. Face ID Enhancements in Low Light Conditions

Face ID has been refined to **work more efficiently in low-light environments**, allowing users to unlock their devices even in dimly lit rooms or nighttime settings.

- **How to enable:** This update applies automatically, ensuring Face ID is more responsive in all lighting conditions.

2. Dual Face ID Profiles

For the first time, iOS 18.4 allows **two different Face ID profiles** on a single device, enabling **multiple users to access a shared iPhone securely**. This is useful for families, business teams, or shared devices.

- **How to set up:**
  1. Go to **Settings** > **Face ID & Passcode**.
  2. Tap **Set Up an Alternate Appearance** and scan the second user's face.
  3. Confirm access permissions and save changes.

3. Auto-Generated Strong Passcodes

Apple now suggests **auto-generated strong passcodes** when setting up a new iPhone or creating a new Apple ID. These passcodes are:

- **Alphanumeric** with a combination of uppercase, lowercase, numbers, and symbols.

- **Unique to each device** to prevent unauthorized access.

- **Encrypted and stored in iCloud Keychain** for secure retrieval.

- **How to enable:** When setting up an iPhone or changing a passcode, iOS will suggest a **strong, unique passcode** automatically.

4. Temporary Passcodes for Shared Access

A new feature allows users to **create temporary passcodes** for trusted friends, family, or employees who may need access to the device for a short period. These passcodes automatically **expire after a set**

duration to prevent unauthorized long-term access.

- **How to enable:**
    1. Go to **Settings** > **Face ID & Passcode**.
    2. Tap **Temporary Passcode** and set an expiration time.

Managing App Tracking, Permissions, and Data Security

Apple continues to emphasize **app transparency and user control**, making it easier to **monitor app permissions, manage tracking, and safeguard personal data**.

1. Real-Time App Tracking Notifications

Users will now receive **real-time alerts** when an app **attempts to track their activity**, allowing them to block tracking immediately.

- **How it works:**
  - When an app requests tracking permissions, iOS displays a **live notification** with an option to **Allow Once** or **Deny Permanently**.
  - Users can review tracking history in **Settings** > **Privacy** > **App Tracking Transparency**.

2. One-Time Permissions for Sensitive Data

Apps that request access to sensitive data (such as **location, microphone, or camera**) now offer **one-time permissions**, meaning access is revoked immediately after the session ends.

- **How to enable:**
  - When an app asks for access, select **Allow Once** instead of **Always Allow.**

3. End-to-End Encryption for iCloud Backups

iOS 18.4 expands **Advanced Data Protection**, ensuring that **iCloud backups, including messages, photos, and notes, are end-to-end encrypted.**

- **How to enable:**
    1. Open **Settings > iCloud > Advanced Data Protection**.
    2. Toggle **On** to encrypt backups.

4. Enhanced Password Manager and Passkeys

The built-in **Password Manager** now provides:

- **Dark web monitoring**, alerting users if their credentials have been exposed in a data breach.

- **Auto-migration to passkeys**, ensuring **phishing-resistant logins** for supported apps and websites.

- **How to use:**

  1. Go to **Settings** > **Passwords**.
  2. Check for any security alerts and update compromised passwords.

With iOS 18.4, Apple has introduced a **powerful set of security and privacy enhancements** that fortify user protection without compromising ease of access. From **stronger Face ID authentication and encrypted backups to enhanced app tracking transparency and on-device AI for privacy**, this update ensures that iPhone users remain **in control of their data at all times**.

By implementing **real-time security notifications,** **customizable authentication options, and next-level encryption**, Apple continues to set the gold standard in **privacy-focused mobile security**. Whether you're safeguarding sensitive information, managing app permissions, or simply looking for a more secure browsing experience, **iOS 18.4 offers a robust suite of tools to keep your device and personal data safe**.

Chapter 5

Enhancements in Apple Apps

With every iOS update, Apple refines its core applications to enhance usability, performance, and overall functionality. iOS 18.4 introduces a range of **powerful upgrades** across **Messages, Safari, Mail, Notes, Photos, Camera, Reminders, Calendar, Files, and more**. These improvements are designed to optimize productivity, elevate communication, and streamline everyday tasks while ensuring **a seamless and intuitive experience**. This chapter explores the **major enhancements in Apple's built-in apps,** highlighting new features and their practical applications.

Updates in Messages, Safari, Mail, and Notes

Apple's most frequently used apps— **Messages, Safari, Mail, and Notes**— have received meaningful refinements that improve communication, browsing, and organization.

1. Messages: Smart Replies, RCS Support, and Animated Reactions

The Messages app has been **significantly upgraded** in iOS 18.4, making texting more **dynamic, secure, and engaging**.

- **Smart Replies:** Apple introduces **AI-powered smart reply suggestions**, allowing users to **quickly respond to texts with contextually relevant responses**.
- **RCS Integration:** Apple has finally enabled **Rich Communication Services (RCS)** for **improved messaging between iPhone and Android users**, providing **higher-quality media sharing, real-time typing indicators, and better group chat experiences**.
- **Animated Reactions:** Users can now react to messages with **custom animated emojis and stickers**, adding a new layer of expression to conversations.

- **Improved Voice Messages:** Transcriptions for voice messages are now more accurate, and users can **adjust playback speed** for quicker listening.

2. Safari: Enhanced Privacy and AI-Powered Search

Safari remains **one of the most secure and efficient web browsers**, and iOS 18.4 takes it a step further with **AI-driven search enhancements and stronger privacy tools**.

- **Intelligent Search Suggestions:** Safari now uses **on-device AI** to provide **smarter search predictions, summarizing web pages before users open them**.

- **Private Browsing Upgrades:** The private browsing mode now automatically **locks inactive tabs** when the iPhone is idle for extended periods.
- **AI-Powered Reader Mode:** Apple has introduced **automatic content summarization in Reader Mode**, allowing users to **see key points from an article at a glance**.
- **Faster Page Loading:** Safari now preloads frequently visited sites and **optimizes performance for ad-heavy pages**.

3. Mail: AI-Powered Categorization and Smart Filters

Apple's Mail app has received a **major overhaul in organization and**

searchability, making it easier to **manage emails efficiently**.

- **AI-Powered Categorization:** Emails are now **automatically sorted into categories like Primary, Promotions, and Updates**, similar to Gmail's tab system.
- **Smart Filters:** Users can now **filter emails based on priority, sender, or unread status**, making inbox navigation smoother.
- **Scheduled Send Improvements:** The **Send Later** feature is now **more customizable**, allowing users to **set precise delivery times**.

4. Notes: Smart Summaries and Handwriting Recognition

Apple's Notes app remains a **powerful tool for organization**, and iOS 18.4 enhances it with **AI-driven summarization and improved handwriting recognition**.

- **Smart Summaries:** Notes can now be **automatically summarized**, providing key takeaways at a glance.
- **Enhanced Handwriting Recognition:** Handwritten notes are now **converted into searchable, formatted text with greater accuracy**.
- **Collaborative Editing Improvements:** Real-time collaboration has been refined, with **easier version tracking and**

improved syncing between devices.

New Features in Photos and Camera

The **Photos and Camera apps** in iOS 18.4 introduce **AI-powered enhancements, better organization tools, and professional-grade camera features**, making it easier to capture and manage memories.

1. Photos: AI-Powered Search and Auto-Generated Albums

- **AI-Powered Search:** The Photos app now allows users to **search images by describing the content in natural language** (e.g., "sunset at the beach" or "dog playing in the park").

- **Auto-Generated Albums:** iOS 18.4 can automatically **create curated photo albums** based on recurring themes, locations, and faces.

- **Improved Duplicate Detection:** The system now identifies **similar photos and suggests the best one based on clarity and composition**.

2. Camera: Pro-Grade Features and Smart Adjustments

- **Auto-Enhance with AI:** The Camera app now **automatically adjusts brightness, contrast, and focus** to produce the best shot in real time.

- **Improved Night Mode:** Night photography has been improved with **better noise reduction and sharper low-light images**.
- **Action Mode Enhancements:** Motion shots are now **stabilized more effectively**, reducing blur when capturing fast-moving subjects.

Productivity Improvements in Reminders, Calendar, and Files

Apple's productivity apps have received powerful refinements in iOS 18.4, making it easier to stay organized, manage tasks, and access important files.

1. Reminders: AI-Powered Task Suggestions and Smart Sorting

- **AI-Powered Task Suggestions:** The app now **analyzes past reminders** and suggests new tasks based on user habits.

- **Smart Sorting:** Reminders are **automatically categorized into relevant lists**, such as Work, Personal, and Shopping.

- **Shared Reminders with Smart Delegation:** Users can now **assign specific tasks to contacts**, integrating seamlessly with the Calendar app.

2. Calendar: Smart Event Detection and Integration with Messages

- **Smart Event Detection:** The Calendar app now **recognizes potential events from Messages, Mail, and Notes** and suggests them as calendar entries.
- **Enhanced Meeting Management:** Users can now **attach documents to calendar events** for easier reference.
- **Improved Time Zone Support:** iOS 18.4 now **automatically adjusts event times based on travel schedules and location changes**.

3. Files: Smarter Organization and AI-Based Search

- **AI-Based File Search:** Users can **find files faster with AI-powered search**, which **understands content inside documents, images, and PDFs**.
- **Improved Cloud Syncing:** Files now sync more efficiently across iCloud, with **less delay and improved offline access**.

Spotlight Search and Siri Advancements

1. Spotlight Search: Smarter AI-Based Results

- **Context-Aware Suggestions:** Spotlight can now predict what you're looking for based on past searches, current activity, and location.
- **Instant Actions:** Users can now take quick actions directly from Spotlight results, such as calling contacts, opening apps, or setting reminders.

2. Siri: AI-Powered Conversations and Personalized Assistance

- **Conversational AI:** Siri now understands longer, more complex commands and responds in a more human-like manner.
- **Cross-App Actions:** Siri can perform multi-step tasks across multiple apps, such as "Remind me to

email Sarah about the budget report when I open Mail."

- **Offline Mode Enhancements:** Siri can now perform more actions without an internet connection, such as setting alarms, adjusting settings, and opening apps.

With iOS 18.4, Apple has introduced **groundbreaking refinements** to its core applications, enhancing **communication, photography, productivity, and AI-driven interactions**. By leveraging **on-device AI, improved search algorithms, and deeper integration between apps**, Apple continues to **push the boundaries of what an iPhone can**

do, making daily tasks more seamless, intuitive, and enjoyable.

Chapter 6

Performance & Battery Life Optimization

Apple's commitment to refining iOS performance is evident in **iOS 18.4**, which brings a host of **speed improvements, battery optimizations, and storage management features**. Whether you're using an **older device** or the latest iPhone, Apple has implemented **efficiency-focused enhancements** that extend battery life, boost responsiveness, and ensure smoother multitasking.

How iOS 18.4 Improves Speed and Efficiency

Apple has optimized iOS 18.4 to **run faster, handle background processes more efficiently, and reduce lag across the system**. Key areas of performance improvement include **app launch speeds, smoother multitasking, and better memory management**.

1. Faster App Launches and Transitions

- iOS 18.4 **reduces app launch times by up to 20%**, making frequently used apps open **almost instantly**.
- Switching between apps is now **smoother**, thanks to **optimized RAM allocation**, preventing

slowdowns even on **older iPhone models**.

- Gestures and animations feel more fluid, with **improved response times when swiping, scrolling, and navigating**.

2. Optimized Background Processes

- Apps running in the background now use **less CPU and battery**, ensuring that performance isn't affected by background tasks.
- **Smarter resource allocation** prioritizes **active applications**, minimizing unnecessary power consumption by idle apps.
- **Adaptive Refresh Rates:** iPhones with **ProMotion displays** dynamically adjust refresh rates based

on user activity, improving **battery efficiency and smoothness**.

3. AI-Powered System Management

- iOS 18.4 introduces **AI-driven system optimizations**, which intelligently learn from **user behavior** to improve efficiency.
- The OS automatically **pauses unused processes and reduces CPU usage when performing low-priority tasks**, extending battery life while maintaining performance.

Battery Health Improvements and Management Techniques

Apple has enhanced **battery longevity and management tools** in iOS 18.4, ensuring that **devices stay powered longer throughout the day**.

1. Improved Battery Efficiency

- iOS 18.4 includes **new power-saving algorithms** that extend battery life by **reducing power-hungry background tasks**.
- **Enhanced Adaptive Charging** helps **prolong battery lifespan** by **learning your charging habits** and slowing down charging when appropriate.
- Apps consuming excessive battery power are now **automatically flagged**, allowing users to **disable**

background activity for specific apps.

2. Smarter Low Power Mode

- **Low Power Mode** has been improved to **dynamically adjust screen brightness, refresh rates, and background tasks**, reducing battery drain more effectively.
- Users can now set **custom schedules** for Low Power Mode, activating it **automatically at a chosen battery percentage or time of day**.

3. Battery Health Insights & Recommendations

- iOS 18.4 introduces **advanced battery health monitoring**, providing more **detailed insights into battery wear and overall capacity**.

- New recommendations appear in Settings, such as **"Consider reducing background app refresh to extend battery life."**

Optimizing Storage and App Performance

Storage management is crucial for maintaining system speed and efficiency, and iOS 18.4 introduces new tools to help users free up space and keep apps running smoothly.

1. Smarter Storage Management

- iOS 18.4 introduces **AI-powered storage optimization**, which **automatically removes temporary files and caches** from apps to free up space.
- The **Offload Unused Apps** feature is now **more proactive**, intelligently removing rarely used apps while keeping **important data intact**.
- **Photo and Video Compression:** The system now **automatically compresses large media files** without noticeable quality loss, helping users save space.

2. Performance-Optimized App Updates

- App updates now require **less storage space and download**

faster, thanks to Apple's **incremental update technology**.

- The system intelligently updates **frequently used apps first**, reducing the impact of updates on overall performance.

3. Faster File Access and Loading Times

- The Files app now loads large documents **significantly faster**, thanks to **improved indexing and caching**.
- Large email attachments and cloud-based files now **open instantly**, as iOS **pre-fetches frequently accessed files in the background**.

With iOS 18.4, Apple has successfully **optimized performance, extended battery life, and refined storage management**, ensuring a **faster, smoother, and more efficient user experience**. Whether you're on **an older iPhone** or the latest model, these improvements ensure that **your device runs at peak efficiency**, minimizing slowdowns and maximizing productivity.

Chapter 7

Troubleshooting & Common Issues

Every new iOS update brings exciting features and improvements, but it can also introduce unexpected issues that impact performance, connectivity, and overall user experience. **iOS 18.4** is no exception. While Apple continuously refines its software to minimize problems, some users may encounter **bugs, crashes, and system glitches** after updating.

This chapter explores the **most common issues users face after installing iOS 18.4, practical solutions to fix them,** and **when a full reset or clean install might be necessary** to restore optimal performance.

Common Problems After Updating and How to Fix Them

Updating to iOS 18.4 should be a seamless experience, but **some users may encounter issues such as battery drain, app crashes, or sluggish performance**. Below are some of the most frequent problems and how to fix them.

1. Battery Draining Faster Than Usual

After updating, your iPhone may experience **increased battery drain** as the system **re-**

indexes data, updates apps, and adjusts to new settings.

How to Fix:

- **Wait 24–48 Hours:** iOS needs time to optimize background processes. If battery life doesn't improve, try the following steps.
- **Check Battery Usage:** Go to **Settings > Battery** to see which apps consume the most power and restrict background activity for those apps.
- **Enable Low Power Mode:** Activate **Low Power Mode** in **Settings > Battery** to reduce background tasks.
- **Turn Off Background App Refresh:** Navigate to **Settings > General > Background App**

Refresh and disable it for non-essential apps.

- **Update All Apps:** Developers often release **compatibility updates** after a major iOS update, which can help resolve battery drain issues.

2. Apps Crashing or Not Opening

Some apps may **fail to open or crash frequently** due to compatibility issues with iOS 18.4.

How to Fix:

- **Restart Your Device:** A simple restart can fix temporary app crashes.
- **Check for App Updates:** Open the **App Store**, go to **Updates**, and install any available updates.

- **Reinstall the App:** Delete the problematic app and reinstall it from the App Store.
- **Reset All Settings:** If the issue persists, go to **Settings > General > Transfer or Reset iPhone > Reset > Reset All Settings** (this won't erase your data).

3. Slow Performance or Lag

Some users report that their iPhone **feels sluggish** after updating. This is often due to background optimization processes.

How to Fix:

- **Restart Your iPhone:** This clears temporary cache and improves speed.

- **Free Up Storage:** Go to **Settings > General > iPhone Storage** and delete unnecessary files and apps.
- **Disable Unused Features:** Reduce animations by enabling **Reduce Motion** in **Settings > Accessibility > Motion**.
- **Turn Off Background Processes:** Close unused apps and disable widgets that consume processing power.

4. Wi-Fi or Cellular Connectivity Issues

After an update, some users experience **Wi-Fi dropping, slow internet speeds, or issues connecting to cellular networks**.

How to Fix:

- **Restart Your Router and iPhone:** Power cycle both devices to refresh the connection.
- **Forget and Reconnect to Wi-Fi:** Go to **Settings** > **Wi-Fi**, tap your network, and select **Forget This Network** before reconnecting.
- **Reset Network Settings:** If problems persist, go to **Settings** > **General** > **Transfer or Reset iPhone** > **Reset** > **Reset Network Settings** (this erases saved Wi-Fi passwords).
- **Check for Carrier Updates:** Go to **Settings** > **General** > **About** and install any available carrier updates.

5. Bluetooth Not Connecting

If Bluetooth devices fail to pair or disconnect frequently, try these solutions.

How to Fix:

- **Turn Bluetooth Off and On:** Go to **Settings > Bluetooth** and toggle it off and on.
- **Forget and Re-Pair Devices:** Tap the device name under **Settings > Bluetooth**, select **Forget This Device**, then re-pair it.
- **Reset Network Settings:** This also resets Bluetooth connections, which may resolve persistent issues.

Resolving Bugs, Crashes, and System Instability

Some users report **random crashes, freezing, or app glitches** after updating to iOS 18.4. These problems often occur due to **corrupt system files, incompatible settings, or background conflicts**.

1. Force Restart Your iPhone

A force restart can **clear temporary glitches** and refresh system processes.

- **For iPhone 8 and later:** Press and quickly release the **Volume Up button**, then the **Volume Down button**. Press and hold the **Side button** until the Apple logo appears.
- **For iPhone 7/7 Plus:** Hold the **Volume Down** and **Power button** together until you see the Apple logo.

- **For iPhone 6s and earlier:** Hold the **Home** and **Power button** together until the Apple logo appears.

2. Check for Software Updates

Apple frequently releases **bug fixes and minor updates** to address issues discovered after major updates.

- Go to **Settings > General > Software Update** and install any available patches.

3. Clear System Cache

Clearing cache helps **fix sluggish performance and frequent crashes**.

- Open **Settings > Safari > Clear History and Website Data** to remove unnecessary cached files.

- Restart your device to refresh system processes.

4. Reset All Settings

If your iPhone continues to **crash or act erratically**, resetting settings can **restore stability without deleting personal data**.

- Go to **Settings > General > Transfer or Reset iPhone > Reset > Reset All Settings**.

When to Reset Settings or Perform a Clean Install

If your device **continues to experience major issues** despite troubleshooting, it may be necessary to **reset all settings or perform a clean install of iOS 18.4**.

1. When to Reset All Settings

Resetting settings **does not delete personal data** but resets system settings like Wi-Fi, notifications, and accessibility preferences.

- Recommended if:
    - Apps frequently **crash or freeze**.
    - Wi-Fi or Bluetooth connections are **unstable**.
    - Performance is **sluggish despite other fixes**.
- To reset all settings:

- Go to Settings > General > Transfer or Reset iPhone > Reset > Reset All Settings.

2. When to Perform a Clean Install

A clean install **erases all data and reinstalls iOS 18.4 from scratch**, resolving deep-rooted system problems.

- Recommended if:
  - You experience **severe crashes, boot loops, or persistent bugs**.
  - Performance remains **unusable after multiple troubleshooting attempts**.
  - You suspect **corrupt system files** are causing issues.
- Steps to Perform a Clean Install:

- Backup Your Data: Use iCloud or a computer to back up everything.

- Put iPhone in Recovery Mode: Connect to a Mac or PC, open Finder (Mac) or iTunes (Windows), then force restart the device until the recovery screen appears.

- Choose "Restore iPhone": This erases all data and installs a fresh copy of iOS 18.4.

- Set Up as New: Avoid restoring from a backup immediately to prevent reintroducing old issues.

While **iOS 18.4 is designed to enhance performance and usability**, some users may encounter **temporary issues** after updating. With **proper troubleshooting**, most problems—whether **battery drain, app crashes, connectivity issues, or system instability**—can be resolved easily.

For persistent issues, **resetting settings or performing a clean install** ensures that your device runs smoothly. By following these solutions, you can **enjoy the best of iOS 18.4 without frustrating interruptions**.

Chapter 8

Tips & Tricks to Maximize Your Experience

With **iOS 18.4**, Apple has refined the user experience, adding new features, shortcuts, and customization options that can make everyday tasks **faster and more efficient**. Many users barely scratch the surface of what their iPhones can do, missing out on **hidden tricks** that can significantly **enhance productivity, multitasking, and convenience**.

Best Practices for Getting the Most Out of iOS 18.4

A few small adjustments can make a big difference in how smoothly and efficiently your iPhone operates. Below are some best practices to help you make the most of iOS 18.4.

1. Keep Your Software Updated

Apple frequently releases **minor updates** to fix bugs, improve security, and optimize performance.

- To check for updates, go to **Settings > General > Software Update** and install any available updates.
- Enable **Automatic Updates** to ensure your iPhone stays up to date without manual intervention.

2. Manage Background Activity to Improve Performance

Background app activity can **slow down your device and drain the battery**.

- Disable **Background App Refresh** for non-essential apps in **Settings > General > Background App Refresh**.
- Restrict apps from **running in the background** by adjusting **Battery Usage settings** under **Settings > Battery**.

3. Organize Your Home Screen for Faster Access

A cluttered home screen slows down navigation. **Use widgets, folders, and the App Library** for a streamlined experience.

- Drag apps into **folders** for better organization.
- Use the **App Library** by swiping left past the last home screen page.
- Add **interactive widgets** for quick access to calendar events, reminders, and weather updates.

4. Customize Focus Modes for a Distraction-Free Experience

With **Focus Mode**, you can filter notifications based on your current activity.

- Go to **Settings > Focus** to create a custom Focus Mode.
- Set different notification preferences for **Work, Sleep, or Personal time**.

- Sync Focus Modes across all Apple devices for seamless transitions.

Shortcuts, Gestures, and Efficiency Hacks

Apple's iOS ecosystem is full of **hidden gestures, shortcuts, and automation tricks** that make navigation faster and more intuitive. Here are some of the most powerful ones.

1. Use Back Tap for Quick Actions

Back Tap lets you perform actions by **double- or triple-tapping the back of your iPhone**.

- Go to **Settings > Accessibility > Touch > Back Tap**.
- Assign actions like **taking a screenshot, opening Control Center, or launching an app**.

2. Swipe Gestures for Faster Navigation

- **Swipe left on notifications** to quickly **clear, mute, or manage them**.
- **Swipe down on the home screen** to access **Spotlight Search** instantly.
- **Swipe right from the lock screen** to launch the **Camera app** in seconds.

3. Master Quick Notes and Drag-and-Drop

- Swipe up from the bottom corner with an **Apple Pencil** or finger to launch **Quick Note**.
- Use **drag-and-drop** to move text, images, and files between apps effortlessly.

4. Automate Tasks with the Shortcuts App

The **Shortcuts app** allows you to create automation routines for everyday tasks.

- Open **Shortcuts** and create a new automation, such as:

- ○ **"Turn on Low Power Mode when the battery drops below 20%."**
- ○ **"Automatically send a message when arriving at a location."**
- Use **pre-made shortcuts** from the Shortcuts Gallery to save time.

Customizing Notifications, Multitasking, and System Preferences

iOS 18.4 introduces enhanced control over notifications, multitasking, and system preferences, allowing for better organization and a smoother workflow.

1. Tame Your Notifications with Advanced Controls

Managing notifications properly can **reduce distractions and improve focus**.

- **Go to Settings > Notifications** to adjust:

    - **Scheduled Summaries**: Receive grouped notifications at set times.
    - **Notification Grouping**: Organize messages by app or thread.
    - **Temporary Banners**: Keep alerts visible only for a few seconds.

- Use **Focus Mode filters** to allow notifications only from selected contacts and apps.

2. Master Multitasking Like a Pro

Multitasking has evolved with new split-screen capabilities and improved app-switching gestures.

- **Use Slide Over and Split View (iPads only)** to run multiple apps side by side.
- **Swipe up and hold** to access the **App Switcher**, making it easy to jump between tasks.
- **Drag-and-drop content between apps** for seamless file sharing.

3. Optimize System Preferences for a Smoother Experience

Fine-tuning system settings can improve performance, privacy, and ease of use.

- **Dark Mode**: Reduce eye strain and save battery by enabling **Dark Mode** in **Settings > Display & Brightness**.
- **One-Handed Mode**: Use **Reachability** (swipe down on the bottom edge) to access the top of the screen easily.
- **Keyboard Shortcuts**: Enable **Slide to Type** or **One-Handed Keyboard** for faster texting.

iOS 18.4 is packed with powerful tools and optimizations that, when fully utilized, can transform how you use your iPhone. By customizing settings, mastering shortcuts, and optimizing multitasking features, you can boost efficiency, streamline navigation, and create a truly personalized experience.

Whether you're looking to increase productivity, reduce distractions, or enhance system performance, these tips and tricks will help you get the most out of iOS 18.4.

Conclusion

With the release of **iOS 18.4**, Apple has once again pushed the boundaries of innovation, refining performance, enhancing security, and introducing new features that make the iPhone experience more **intuitive, efficient, and powerful**. Whether you've explored the **major upgrades, hidden features, customization options, or security enhancements**, one thing is clear—this update is designed to make your device work smarter and seamlessly adapt to your needs.

Key Takeaways

From the moment you installed **iOS 18.4**, you unlocked a new level of functionality. Some of the **most important highlights** from this guide include:

- **A streamlined user experience** with design tweaks, UI refinements, and smoother multitasking.
- **Stronger security and privacy measures** that put you in control of your data.
- **Enhanced system apps**, including improved messaging, smarter search, and a more powerful Siri.
- **Performance and battery optimizations** that improve device longevity and efficiency.

- **Hidden features and customization options** that allow for a truly personalized iPhone experience.

Whether you're a casual user or a power user, **iOS 18.4 ensures that your iPhone adapts to your lifestyle**, offering both simplicity and advanced capabilities.

Staying Updated with Future iOS Releases

Technology evolves rapidly, and Apple continues to refine and enhance iOS with new features, security patches, and performance optimizations. To stay ahead and make the most of your iPhone, consider the following:

- **Enable automatic updates** in *Settings > General > Software Update* to ensure you always have the latest enhancements.

- **Follow Apple's official announcements** through Apple's website, WWDC events, and keynote presentations to stay informed about upcoming features.

- **Join Apple's Beta Program** if you want early access to new features before they are publicly released.

- **Engage with the iPhone community** through forums, blogs, and Apple support channels to discover user insights, troubleshooting tips, and creative ways to use new features.

Enjoy Your iPhone to the Fullest

An iPhone isn't just a device—it's an extension of your lifestyle, your work, and your creativity. With iOS 18.4, you now have access to more powerful tools, smarter automation, and deeper customization that allow you to tailor your device to match your unique preferences.

As you continue to explore all that this update has to offer, remember that the **best way to unlock your iPhone's full potential is to experiment, personalize, and take advantage of the innovations Apple provides**.

Whether you're navigating daily tasks with greater ease, fine-tuning your settings for maximum efficiency, or simply enjoying the seamless integration of Apple's ecosystem, **iOS 18.4 is designed to enhance your experience in every way**.

So go ahead—**dive into the possibilities, try new features, and enjoy your iPhone like never before!**